My first Internet guide

Chris Oxlade

Heinemann
LIBRARY

www.heinemann.co.uk/library
Visit our website to find out more information about Heinemann Library books.

To order:
☎ Phone 44 (0) 1865 888066
🖹 Send a fax to 44 (0) 1865 314091
🖥 Visit the Heinemann Bookshop at www.heinemann.co.uk/library to browse our catalogue and order online.

First published in Great Britain by Heinemann Library, Halley Court, Jordan Hill, Oxford OX2 8EJ, part of Harcourt Education.
Heinemann is a registered trademark of Harcourt Education Ltd.

Editorial: Isabel Thomas, Charlotte Guillain and Diyan Leake
Design: Philippa Jenkins
Illustrations: Tower Designs (UK) Ltd
Picture Research: Melissa Allison
Production: Duncan Gilbert

Originated by Dot Gradations
Printed and bound in China by South China Printing Co. Ltd

ISBN 978 0 431 90697 3 (hardback)
11 10 09 08 07
10 9 8 7 6 5 4 3 2 1

ISBN 978 0 431 90702 4 (paperback)
12 11 10 09 08
10 9 8 7 6 5 4 3 2 1

British Library Cataloguing in Publication Data
Oxlade, Chris
  My first Internet guide. - (My First Computer Guides)
  1. Internet - Juvenile literature 2. World Wide Web - Juvenile literature
  I. Title
  004.6'78

A full catalogue record for this book is available from the British Library.

Acknowledgements
The publishers would like to thank the following for permission to reproduce photographs: © The Natural History Museum, London p. 13; Courtesy of NASA p. 24 right; Courtesy of World Book, Inc. p. 17; Getty Images pp. 5 (Taxi), 20 inset (Photodisc); Harcourt Education Ltd pp. 7 top (Heinemann Explore), 7, 20, 25 top, 26, 27 (Tudor Photography); Internet Explorer is a registered trade mark of Microsoft Corporation in the United States and United Kingdom p. 8 left; Mozilla.org p. 8 right; The screen capture taken from pbskids.org contains copyrighted material of the Public Broadcasting Service. p.6 lower right; © 2007 Crayola. Crayola®, Oval Smile Design®, Color Explosion™, Chevron Design™, used with permission. p. 6 left; http://www.kidsnewsroom.org p. 18; http://www.kids-space.org p. 6 top right; Imagestate Royalty-Free p. 16; Lexmark International p. 21; NaturePL/Anup Shah p. 23; Superstock pp. 19 (Francisco Cruz), 29 (J Silver)

Cover photograph of USB2 cable hub, close-up, reproduced with permission of Getty Images (Photodisc Red).

The publishers would like to thank Robert Eiffert for his assistance in the preparation of this book.

Every effort has been made to contact copyright holders of any material reproduced in this book. Any omissions will be rectified in subsequent printings if notice is given to the publishers.

Contents

Some words are shown in bold, **like this**. You can find out what they mean by looking in the glossary.

What is the Internet?

The Internet is made up of millions of computers all over the world. The computers are all linked together so they can swap information.

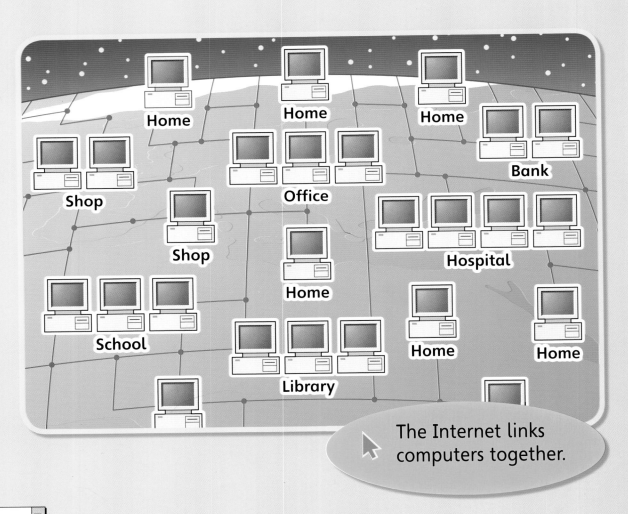

Home

Home

Home

Bank

Shop

Office

Shop

Hospital

School

Home

Home

Home

Library

The Internet links computers together.

You can find out about almost any subject on the Internet.

The Internet lets us look at information stored on other computers. It also lets us communicate with each other using **email**.

What is a website?

A website is made up of information stored on the Internet. The screens that you see are called web pages. All the web pages together are called the World Wide Web, or **www** for short.

There are millions and millions of websites on the Internet.

Web pages can be made up of text, photographs, pictures, sounds, and video. Pages in books can only show text and pictures.

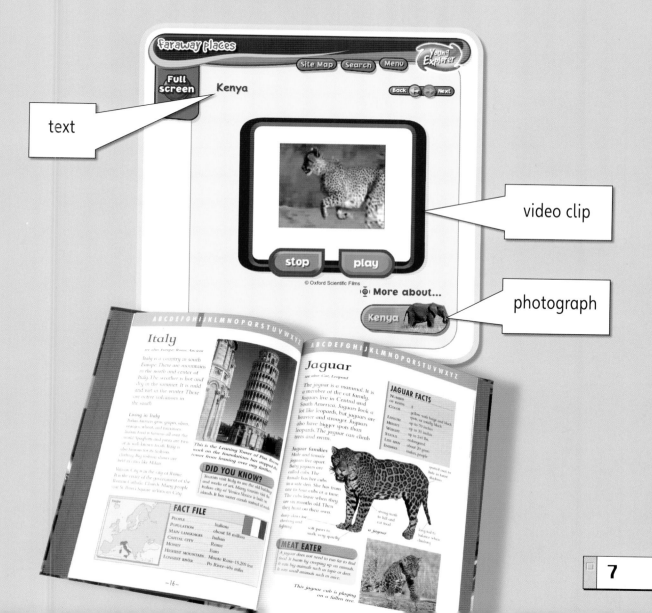

text

video clip

photograph

Web browsers

You need a special **program** on your computer to look at websites. This kind of program is called a **web browser**. There are many types of web browser.

Click on the picture of the web browser to start the program.

Internet Explorer   Firefox

To see a web page, you put its address into the address bar in a web browser. Then you press the "Enter" key. The web page loads, or opens, on to your computer. This may take a few seconds.

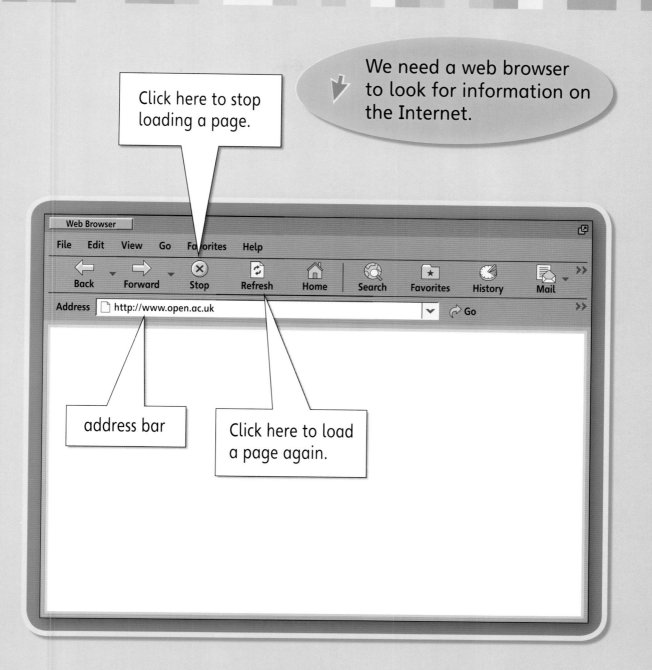

Click here to stop
loading a page.

We need a web browser
to look for information on
the Internet.

Web Browser

File   Edit   View   Go   Favorites   Help

Back   Forward   Stop   Refresh   Home   Search   Favorites   History   Mail

Address   http://www.open.ac.uk   Go

address bar

Click here to load
a page again.

The right address

Every website on the Internet has its own address. Most web addresses begin with **www**. They end with letters like .com or .org.

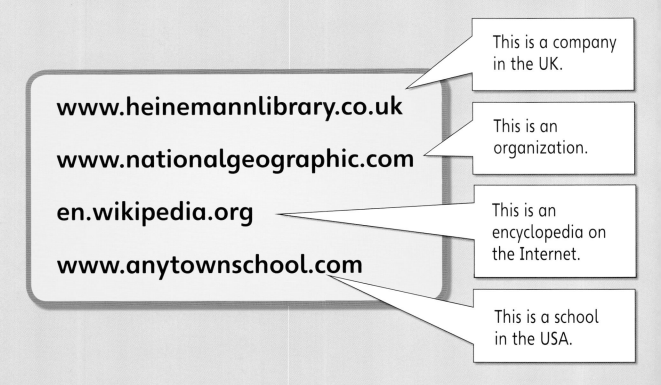

www.heinemannlibrary.co.uk — This is a company in the UK.

www.nationalgeographic.com — This is an organization.

en.wikipedia.org — This is an encyclopedia on the Internet.

www.anytownschool.com — This is a school in the USA.

The address of the website appears in the address bar at the top of the page. You must type the address in carefully or your computer will not be able to find the web page.

Activity

Look at your favourite comic or magazine. See if you can find the address of its website. It will probably be on the front page.

Web pages

Websites normally have lots of different pages. Each page has different information on it.

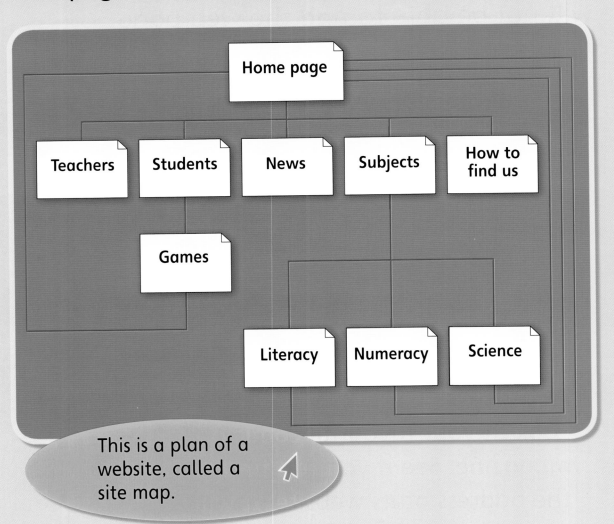

This is a plan of a website, called a site map.

Every website has a **home page**. This is normally the first page you see when you visit a site.

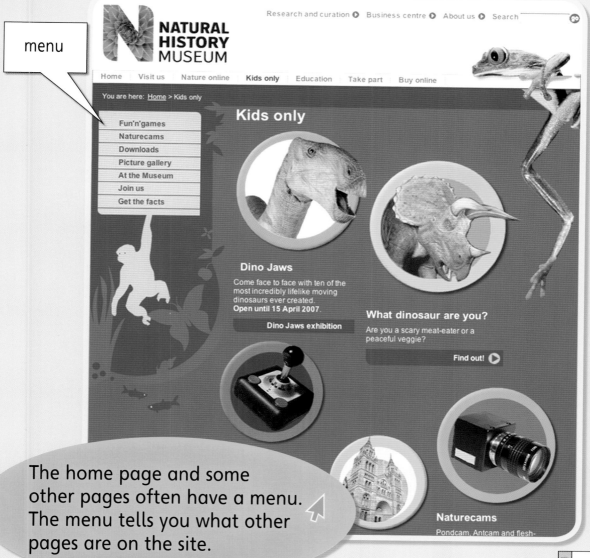

menu

The home page and some other pages often have a menu. The menu tells you what other pages are on the site.

Jumping about

To get from one web page to another you click on words or pictures. These are called **hyperlinks**.

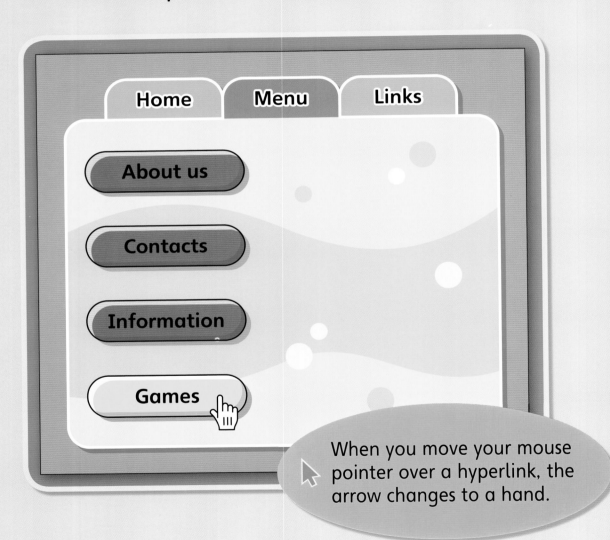

Home Menu Links

About us

Contacts

Information

Games

When you move your mouse pointer over a hyperlink, the arrow changes to a hand.

It can be easy to get lost in a website. You can always get back to the **home page** of a website by clicking on the "Home" button.

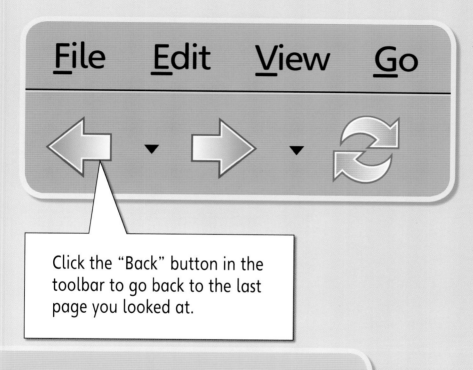

Click the "Back" button in the toolbar to go back to the last page you looked at.

Activity

Try looking at the website of the comic or magazine you found earlier. Is it easy to jump between the pages?

What can I find?

You can visit millions of different websites on the Internet. There are websites about almost anything you can think of.

There are many websites that work like encyclopedias, dictionaries, and atlases.

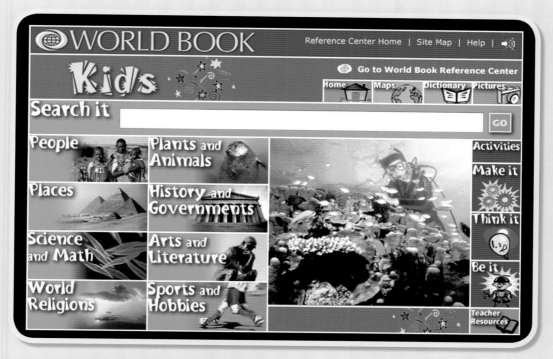

STAY SAFE X

⚠ Some websites are not for children. Always ask an adult if it is okay to visit a site.

News and entertainment

There are many news websites. You can read about the latest news. You can also look at news stories from the past. The best news websites are run by newspapers and television companies.

Some websites are just for fun. There are websites that let you listen to music and watch videos. There are also thousands of websites where you can find out about the latest computer games.

 STAY SAFE

Never type in your name, email address or home address when you are visiting a website. You do not know who will use the information.

Find out!

You can find out information for school projects on the Internet. Ask your teacher or your school librarian for a list of websites about a subject. Or you could look in books about the subject to find some websites to visit. You can also use a **search engine**. Find out how on page 22.

Bengal Tiger Facts
- Bengal tigers live to be about 15 years old in the wild.
- A tiger can eat more than your weight in meat in one meal.
- No two tigers have the same stripe patterns. Each tiger's stripes are different.
- There are about 40 white Bengal tigers in zoos across the world.

More Books to Read
Bengal Tiger, Edana Eckart (Children's Press, 2003)
Bengal Tiger, Richard Spilsbury (Heinemann, 2004)
Bengal Tiger, Rod Theodorou (Heinemann, 2001)

Web Sites
To find out more about charities that help tigers, visit their web sites:
WWF: www.wwf.org
Save the Tiger: www.savethetigerfund.org

Glossary
Asia the largest continent in the world
carnivore animal that eats meat from other animals
continent large area of land divided into different countries
cub baby tiger
extinct when all the animals in a species die out and the species no longer exists
female animal that can become a mother when it grows up. Women and girls are female people.
habitat place where plants and animals grow and live. A forest is a kind of habitat.
mammal animal that feeds its baby with the mother's milk and has some hair on its body
mate what male and female animals do to make babies
poacher someone who hunts animals when it is against the law to do so
reserve area of land where animals are protected and their habitat looked after
species group of animals that look similar and can have babies together
WWF charity that used to be called the World Wildlife Fund

31

Web Sites
To find out more about charities that help tigers, visit their web sites:
WWF: www.wwf.org
Save the Tiger: www.savethetigerfund.org

Always ask your teacher or another adult before printing things out.

Look at a few websites about the subject. Then print out the best pages. Read the information, then write your project. Never copy text from a website and say that it is your own.

Searching the Web

To find out about a subject, you use a special website called a **search engine**. You type **keywords** into the search engine. The search engine searches through millions of websites and gives you a list of websites that might help you.

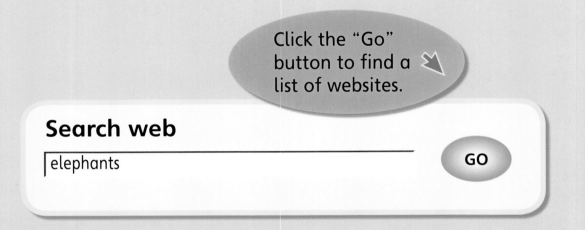

Click the "Go" button to find a list of websites.

Search web

elephants

GO

If you use just one keyword, you might get a list of millions of websites. Try to use two or three keywords at the same time. Then the search engine will give you fewer sites.

Activity

Go to a computer and try searching for information about African elephant babies. Use the keyword "elephants" first. Then use "African elephant" to get fewer results. Then try "African elephant baby".

1. **African** Savannah: **African** Elephant
   African Savannah: **African** Elephant **African** Savannah: **African** Elephant
   Category: Mammals > **African Elephants**
   www.oaklandzoo.org/atox/azeleph.html – More from this site

2. WWF - **African elephants**
   Elephants continue to roam the **African** land, ... addressed in order to conserve **African elephants** and dinimish the factors that threaten them. ...
   panda.org/about_wwf/what_we_do/specia/ .../**african_elephants**/index.cfm - 45k - Cached - More from this site.

3. **African Elephants** - National Zoo FONZ
   ... living mammals, are versatile, enabling **elephants** to manipulate tiny objects or ... **African elephants** communicate with rumbles, growls, bellows, and **moans.**   nationalzoo.si.edu/Animals/African Savanna/fact-afelephant.cfm - 31k - Cached - More from this site

Right or wrong?

Not all the information you find on the Internet is correct. Try to use websites you can trust. The sites of well-known organizations are best.

Space website

Hi!
I am Mike. This is my very own web site. Iv'e learned all about the planets and that, and wont to share it with you all.

This is the moon. They sed it was made of cheeese cos its got lots of hole in it. The earth goes round and round it, and we only see it at night when its dark.

It is the nearest planet to the ea and in the 1960s a guy called Buzz went there in a rockit with some o guys to see what was there, but th did not find nothing.

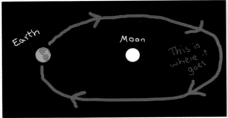

Here are two websites about space. Which would you trust?

Click here to add a website to your list of pages you might want to see again.

When you find a good website, you might want to go back to it another day. Add it to your list of favourite sites. Or look in your **web browser's** "History" menu.

The "History" menu shows you which websites you have visited recently.

History

View ▼ 🔍 Search

📁 www.heinemann.co.uk

📁 www.bbc.co.uk

📁 www.nasa.gov

📁 www.thebritishmuseum.ac.uk

📁 www.sciencemuseum.org.uk

More information sources

The Internet is not the only place to look for information on a subject. You can look up many subjects on CDs or DVDs. Encyclopedia CDs and DVDs have information on almost every subject.

When you look for information on a CD or DVD encyclopedia, you can search using **keywords**. Or you can look up the subject you want in the index.

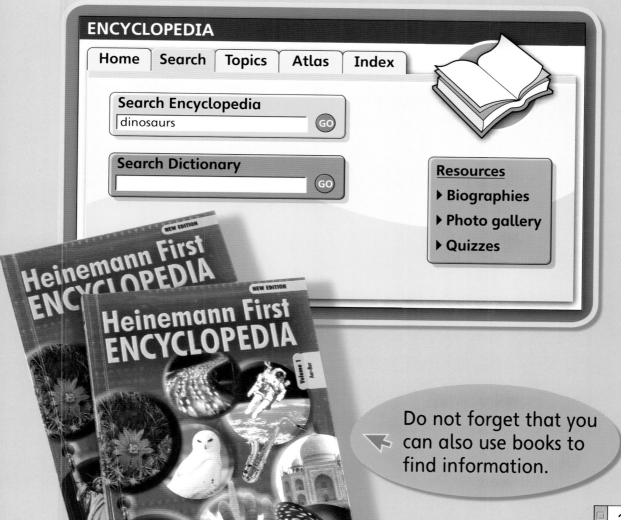

Do not forget that you can also use books to find information.

More Internet uses

Looking at websites is just one of the things you can do on the Internet. The other main thing we do on the Internet is send **emails** to each other.

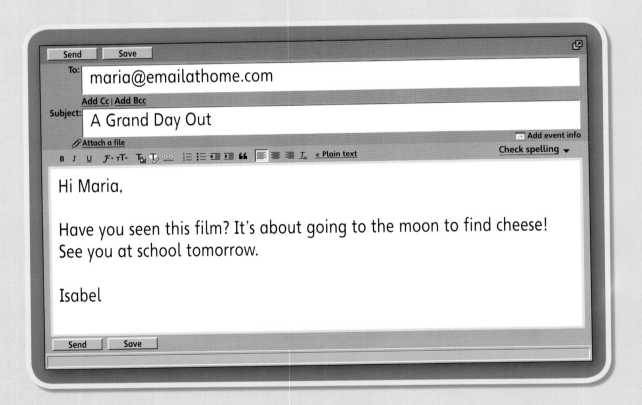

Send   Save

To: maria@emailathome.com

Add Cc | Add Bcc

Subject: A Grand Day Out

Attach a file

Add event info

Check spelling ▾

B I U ꞙ-ₜT- T₈T₇ ∞ ⫶≡ ⫶≡ ⫷≣ ⫸≣ 66 ≣ ≣ ≣ Tₓ « Plain text

Hi Maria,

Have you seen this film? It's about going to the moon to find cheese!
See you at school tomorrow.

Isabel

Send   Save

You can also talk to people on the Internet using instant messaging. Always take care when you use the Internet. Never give your email address, phone number or address to a stranger.

We can use the Internet for work or fun.

Fun facts about the Internet

- The first type of Internet, called the ARPANET, was used in 1969.

- People have been shopping on the Internet since the mid-1990s. Amazon.com was one of the first shopping websites.

More books to read

Learn ICT: Communicate Online, Anne Rooney (QED, 2004)

Shooting Stars: Communication Crazy, Anne Rooney (Chrysalis, 2003)

Glossary

email electronic mail messages sent between computers using the Internet

home page page that introduces a website and shows what the website is about

hyperlink word or picture that links to another web page

keyword important word that describes a subject you want information about

program set of instructions that tells a computer what to do

search engine special website that helps you find information about other websites

web browser program that finds the web pages you want to see

www World Wide Web, made up of millions of websites

Index